The Skateboarder's Guide to
Skate Parks, Half-Pipes, Bowls, and Obstacles™

TAKING ACTION

How to Get Your City to Build a Public Skate Park

Justin Hocking

rosen central™

The Rosen Publishing Group, Inc., New York

To Matt and Sean

Published in 2005 by The Rosen Publishing Group, Inc.
29 East 21st Street, New York, NY 10010

First Edition

Library of Congress Cataloging-in-Publication Data

Hocking, Justin. Taking action: how to get your city to build a public skate park/by Justin Hocking.
    p. cm.—(The skateboarder's guide to skate parks, half-pipes, bowls, and obstacles)
Includes bibliographical references and index.
ISBN 1-4042-0341-9 (library binding)
1. Skateboarding parks—United States—Juvenile literature. 2. Municipal finance—United States—Juvenile literature.
I. Title. II. Series: Hocking, Justin. Skateboarder's guide to skate parks, half-pipes, bowls, and obstacles.
GV859.8.H63 2004
796.22–dc22
                         2004004416

Manufactured in the United States of America

On the cover: Skaters petitioning to have a skate park built

CONTENTS

INTRODUCTION

After psyching yourself up for weeks, you decide that Saturday's the day to try your first grind on the five-stair handrail at your favorite skate spot. You can barely sit still during school on Friday. It's hard to pay attention to your science teacher's lesson on Newton's laws of motion when all you can think about is defying the laws of physics on your skateboard.

You can hardly sleep that night, and when you finally do fall asleep, you dream about skateboarding. In your dream, you

Although skateboarding has been popular for decades, many towns and cities still view skateboarders as a nuisance and prohibit them from using sidewalks and open spaces.

snap a perfect ollie and lock both trucks squarely on the rail, then effort-lessly glide down the whole length, almost like you're flying.

Saturday morning finally arrives. After a quick breakfast, you grab your skateboard and head out the door. A few friends join you along the way, and you all roll as fast as you can toward the skate spot. But once you get there, you can't believe what you see. Someone has posted those annoying "No Skateboarding!" signs all over your spot. And then it gets even worse—you realize that little metal "skatestopper" knobs have been welded to the handrail, making your dream grind impossible.

If you love to skateboard, then you've probably experienced something similar to this disappointing scene. It's called getting shut down, and it's pretty much a daily occurrence for most skaters.

As you may know, skaters sometimes receive hefty fines for skating where they're not supposed to, and some even have their boards taken away by the police. However, many local governments are beginning to recognize this growing problem, and thousands of cities across the country have worked with skateboarders to create one workable solution: public skate parks.

In fact, skate parks are popping up at an amazing rate. According to Consolidated Skateboard Company's *The Plan*, an informative booklet that lays out a basic "plan" for getting a skate park built, there are currently hundreds of skate parks under construction all across the United States, Canada, and other parts of the world. More skate parks were built in the past few years than in the previous twenty.

Still, many cities and towns fail to support their local youth by providing them with an adequate, legal, and fun space for skating. Maybe you live in such a place and have always dreamed about having a good place to skate, a spot where you and your friends can practice doing what you love without getting shut down. If this is the case, you *can* do something about it.

Most existing skate parks were built because skateboarders, their parents, and other community members joined together, took action, and made their dream of a public skate park a reality. This book is designed to help you take all the necessary steps to realize your dreams, including tips on getting organized, creating a petition drive, fund-raising, designing a park, and staying involved.

CHAPTER 1

Getting Organized

The whole process of asking your local government for a public skate park can take months and even years. It takes patience and persistence to overcome the many challenges you may face along the way. But once you actually have a good place to skate with your friends, it's all worth it. You'll feel a great sense of accomplishment from making your ideas and dreams come alive.

Skate park activism has many other rewards, too. You'll create lasting connections with tons of smart and interesting people, including other skaters, parents, politicians, company presidents, and city planners. While working with these people through all the different stages of skate park planning and design, you might even learn something about public speaking, business, art, architecture, and graphic design. You'll also discover a lot about city governments and how they operate. And you'll

The first step in making your town skateboard-friendly is to organize a group and discuss the changes you want to see. A group makes it easier to do research, circulate petitions, start letter-writing campaigns, and come up with solutions that work for everyone.

witness firsthand how a group of determined citizens can actually make their community a better place. This may motivate you to get involved with other community-building projects in the future.

So How Do You Get Started?

The first step is a simple and fun thing that you do all the time: hang out and talk with your friends. Express your vision for a new skate park to everyone you know. It's a pretty good bet that other skaters in your neighborhood have similar ideas but just don't know where to begin. All it really takes to

A SUCCESS STORY

In Fort Collins, Colorado, a group of skateboarders, parents, and the owners of a local skate shop called the Skateboard Market formed a group called the Colorado Amateur Skateboard Association (CASA). In the mid-1990s, they successfully convinced the city government to build a small, temporary skate park at a local recreation center. This park consisted of several wooden ramps and obstacles on an asphalt surface.

In the late 1990s, after realizing that the existing park was too small and outdated to accommodate the growing number of local skateboarders, the members of CASA again pooled their efforts. In 2000, at the request of CASA, the city of Fort Collins constructed a much larger and more modern skate facility—a cement structure consisting mainly of bowls, a snake run, and a street course—at the Edora Recreation Center.

Then, in 2003, the city built yet another public skate park—this one consisting entirely of street-oriented obstacles (things like curbs, ledges, and rails that you might actually encounter in a real street)—at the Fossil Creek Recreation Center. With three excellent facilities, including the Northside Aztlan Community Center, spread throughout a city of more than 100,000 people, Fort Collins is proof that a city is willing to support skateboarders of all ages and levels.

make positive changes in the world is someone like you who can get people organized and give them some direction toward a common goal.

Once you round up a good-sized crew of friends and acquaintances, choose a place to meet, such as your local skate shop. This will be a spot where you can get together regularly and start brainstorming ideas. These first meetings should be fun and informal. This is a good time to tap into your imagination and visualize how great it would be to have your own place to skate.

Most experienced skaters picture themselves landing a trick before they actually attempt it. Likewise, getting together with friends and imagining a new skate park will help you actually achieve your goals. Make sure everyone's voice gets heard during the meetings and designate one member to take notes.

Once you've organized a group of your peers and held a couple of meetings, it's time to approach each group member's parents. Make it clear that you need their help to do something positive for the community. Parents will be some of your most important allies. They know how to get things done, and they'll most likely become your official spokespeople. At this point, you might also choose a name for your newly formed organization.

Now that your group has a name and the support of local parents, ask them to help you approach other key members of the community. Your organization will be most effective if its members include a diverse group of citizens from a variety of ages and backgrounds. You might ask members of some of the following citizen groups to join your team.

Teachers and School Officials

Considering that you see your teachers just about every day, they're probably the most convenient group to first approach for support. Explain that you're hoping not only to get a public skate park built, but also to learn a lot through the process. Teachers are usually good public speakers, not to mention they're great at keeping people (especially young people) organized while they juggle multiple tasks. Who knows, your community activism project might impress your teachers enough that they'll give you some extra credit.

Local Business Owners

The owners and employees of local skate shops are usually older, more experienced skateboarders who can prove to be very important in your quest. Make sure to include them, but don't stop there. You might be

Your local city council meets regularly at a town hall or government building. Many of those meetings are open to citizens who want to make a complaint or a proposal, and that's when you and your group can make the case for better skateboarding facilities in your town.

surprised how many other business owners will support a group of motivated and creative young people.

Most adult businesspeople don't dislike skateboarding, but they may be concerned about the damage it can sometimes cause to public and private property. Convince them that a skate park is an excellent solution to this issue. The more business owners you can get involved, the better. They often have strong connections with local government officials, and they'll also be very helpful once you start fund-raising.

Local Politicians

Getting local politicians on your side is probably the most important move you can make. Ask a parent to help you contact people like city council members, the mayor, and most important, the local parks and recreation department. You'll be much more likely to gain their support if you present some well-researched statistics about the popularity and safety of skate parks (see the statistics sidebar on page 22).

Police

Part of a police officer's job is to keep people and their property safe. This sometimes involves issuing citations for activities like skateboarding. However, most police officers probably don't enjoy writing tickets for these kinds of petty violations. In fact, many of them will understand the root of the problem—that there's no place for skaters to do what they do best—and they'll likely be willing to help you create a solution.

Skaters and police are sometimes at odds. However, if the law is on your side and you're not causing noise or vandalism, the police will respect your right to skateboard.

For instance, in places such as Windham, Maine, the local police department has actually headed a successful campaign to create a public skate park. And it has since noticed a big drop in the amount of skateboarding violations in its town's business district.

Religious Leaders

People such as rabbis, priests, and ministers are concerned with the well-being of young people. Regardless of your own religious background, your skate park campaign will benefit from the support of such well-respected figures. Explain to them how skateboarding is a positive force in your life, one that gives you a great sense of direction and meaning.

11

CHAPTER 2

Creating a Petition Drive

After creating an actual organization of skaters, parents, and important public figures, the next step is to win support from your town's larger population. Once you begin to approach the local city government with your ideas (we'll discuss this in the next chapter), local officials will be much more willing to hear you out if you can prove that a large number of local citizens would like to see a public skate park in their community. The best way to demonstrate this kind of proof is through a petition drive.

What Is a Petition?

When you get right down to it, a petition is nothing more than a short and very convincing letter endorsing a cause that's signed by more than one person. You're

Petitioning is hard work. For the best results, you should do it during the early evenings or weekends, when people are home. Be able to say what you are petitioning for clearly and simply, and be polite and respectful. Be prepared to answer questions about the details of your plan. You may be surprised by how many people in your town will be willing to support your cause.

probably thinking that a simple letter, even one that's been signed by hundreds of people, can't really accomplish much. But some pretty astonishing stuff started with petitions. Thomas Jefferson whipped one up back in 1776, and then found fifty-six like-minded people to sign it. This petition was known, of course, as the Declaration of Independence, and its powerful plea for freedom, justice, and human equality is the basis on which our entire country was built. One of the signers' names, John Hancock, even became a nickname for signatures themselves.

SAMPLE PETITION STATEMENT

We, the undersigned citizens, parents, and skateboarders of (name of your city) wish to express our support for local youth by proposing the construction of a public skate park. Skateboarding is one of the most popular youth activities in the country, and it's time that we provide the underserved skaters in our own community with a safe place to challenge and express themselves.

During the past ten years, hundreds of successful publicly funded skate parks have been constructed in cities and towns across the United States. Not only have they proven to be statistically safer than a basketball court or a public pool, they're also an excellent way to get young people involved in civic and community development.

Young people need to have a sense of ownership in and connection to the community in which they live. A skate park is a great way to build such bridges. Rather than giving young people tickets for participating in a sport they love, let's provide them with a legal place to skate, the same way the city currently provides participants with baseball fields and basketball courts. By organizing and beginning to lobby for a public skate park, these young local skateboarders have already shown a great deal of initiative, creativity, and responsibility. Let's not ignore this opportunity to fulfill an important need and strengthen our community.

Informing the Public

In order to get people to give you their own John Hancock, you'll have to provide them with plenty of information about your cause. So your first task is to put together an information page that briefly explains what your organization is all about and what goals you're trying to achieve. Include anything you think might be relevant and persuasive, such as important statistics and facts about skate parks, quotes, and maybe even

Online petitions are one way to reach people who are missed during door-to-door drives. If you have a good e-mail list, you can send them a link and ask them to sign it. Be aware, however, that only people who live in your area should sign your petition. Your local government is going to be mostly concerned with the opinions of the people who vote for them, not those of the people who live outside the local area.

photos of existing skate parks in other towns. Remember that the best way to win people's support is by proving how a public skate park will directly benefit young people and the community in general. Make sure to include your organization's name and contact information, and make plenty of copies to distribute.

Once you provide people with information about skate parks, the next task is to get their signatures. In order to do this, you'll first need to create signature pages (with numbered lines to make counting easier), as well as a formal petition statement. Feel free to copy or adapt our sample petition on page 14 for your own petition drive.

Getting Signatures

Once you have all your petition materials ready, it's time to go public! You can leave copies of your petition for people to sign at skate shops, libraries, schools, and businesses. But always make sure to ask whomever's in charge for permission to leave a petition at their place of business. You might also consider creating an online petition. Check out www.petitiononline.com for more information.

However, the best way to get the most signatures is by asking for them in person. You can go door to door (accompanied by a parent), but we suggest you try setting up a table outside a skate shop, school, grocery store, the mall, or any place where you're likely to find lots of people (parents are especially good). Consider creating a colorful banner or sign with your organization's name and logo in order to draw attention to your information table.

Make sure signers print, as well as sign, their entire name on your signature pages. You should also research any other petition rules set by your local government. Most cities, for example, won't consider a signature valid unless it includes at least a home address. And they often won't count the names of nonresidents or people not registered to vote.

Be polite and professional to everyone you approach. Along with collecting signatures, it's likely that you'll meet people willing to provide further support to your cause or even to join your organization. Also, once you've collected a significant amount of signatures, consider sending copies of your petition to the local press. An article in a local newspaper will definitely help you spread the word and gain support and may even give you a certain amount of credibility with the city.

CHAPTER 3
Attending City Council Meetings

Once you've collected 100 or more signatures, it's time to take one of the biggest and most important steps in the whole process: approaching the city. Even if every single citizen in your town supports the idea of a new skate park, your plan will go nowhere unless you win the city government's support.

There are several ways your organization can go about doing this. For instance, a small group of parents might be able to set up a meeting with the mayor or one of his or her assistants. However, most cities' parks and recreation departments hold open forum meetings, during which members of the public can voice their opinions and concerns. This sort of meeting is usually the best opportunity for presenting your case.

Putting up billboards or signs advertising your drive for a skate park is a good way to get publicity for your cause. Just be sure you have the right permits to post them and permission from the owner for anything that's posted on private property.

Winning Support

There are many ways to win support at city council and parks and recreation meetings. One way is to have a parent help you do some research to find out time and date information for upcoming meetings. Make sure to show up early so you'll have plenty of time to get everyone organized.

Also, get as many people as possible to show up at these meetings and voice their support for a public skate park. Your goal is to make a serious impression on the city council and any members of the press who

WORKING TOGETHER

"The fact is, you have to work within the system to change it. You have to do things the way the city does, not just the way you do. Don't get frustrated, sometimes government takes a long time to move, but as long as you keep fighting for your rights as citizens, they can't ignore you. But it takes someone to get the ball rolling, and to keep pushing. We hope it's you."

—From Consolidated Skateboard Company's *The Plan*

might attend these meetings. You want to prove that your organization represents a large section of the population and that you actually mean business.

Spread the word among your friends several weeks before the scheduled date. Pass out informative fliers at school that include the time and date of the meeting. Make posters and hang them around your school, the library, telephone poles, community bulletin boards, restaurants, or any other highly visible places. Consider sending out an informative mailer to all the people who included their address when they signed your petition, or place a small ad in a local newspaper. And definitely make sure that everyone in your organization shows up—all the other skaters, parents, businesspeople, police officers, teachers, and any other adults sympathetic to your cause.

It's important to be highly organized during these public meetings. In open forum meetings, each individual is usually given about three minutes to talk. That's really not much time. So beforehand, you should designate individual group members to discuss separate issues. Each person should bring up a different point, such as statistics or quotes that prove there's a need for a skate park in your town, possible positive effects of a skate park on the community, examples of other successful parks, and so on. This way, you'll sound more professional, and you won't end up simply repeating each other.

You should also encourage your adult organization members, especially local businesspeople, to voice their own unique reasons for supporting a public skate park. Finally, don't forget to present all the signatures from your petition drive.

City Council Meetings

City council meetings can be really long and really boring, and you may have to sit through hours of discussion about dull subjects. Even if you get bored, it's important to be polite, professional, and quiet if it's not your turn to talk.

Once you take the stage yourself, you need to sell your ideas to the council members. It might help to think of yourself as sort of a salesperson whose task is to convince the city that your "product" is something their city can't do without. Like a good salesperson, you'll definitely need to consider your audience's values and concerns. As members of an elected body, they want to satisfy all of the community's needs while making the best use of taxpayers' dollars. So you'll have to convince them that a skate park will accomplish both of these things and more.

For instance, in a telephone interview, Matt Day, the landscape architect of the city of Fort Collins, Colorado, who has overseen the construction of two new skate parks in the past few years, said the best way to persuade your city government to build a skate park is to "show the need. Most cities build recreational facilities, parks, and sports fields based on need. You

Every citizen has the right to stand up and voice his or her concerns or support proposals at a city council meeting. But if you're not prepared, you won't convince your audience. Know exactly what you're going to say, bring facts and figures to back up your case, and be concise and to the point. The more professional you sound, the more impact your words will have.

have to compete with a recreational system that is trying to make sure that there are enough ball fields and tennis courts out there. You have to show them that there is an uncerserved section of the population. Changing recreational trends show that isolation sports are gaining on the team sports. Try to use these numbers and statistics to your advantage. Get a good handle on the number of skaters in the area and how they are lacking facilities. Compare them directly to the number of other users and related facilities. Show positive examples of successful public skateboard projects."

21

IMPORTANT STATISTICS

- Skateboarding is growing faster than mountain biking, golfing, and fifty other sports tracked by the National Sporting Goods Association.

- American Sports Data, an online data-collection service, estimates that the number of skateboarders between twelve and eighteen years of age will reach 9.3 million by 2005 in America.

- The U.S. Consumer Product Safety Commission found that skateboarding is statistically safer than football, baseball, soccer, and ice hockey.

- The average skateboarder skates 50.8 days a year. That's almost two months!

Keep in mind that this process will take quite a bit of time. Just like no one ever lands a trick the very first time he or she tries it, the city most likely will not magically grant you a skate park after your first meeting. Council members may consider doing further research into the matter, after which they'll probably think it over for a while before taking a vote on whether or not to have another vote. After some more time thinking it over and a couple more votes, they might actually take a final vote. Does this sound complicated and time consuming? It is. Like we said earlier, you may have to attend many of these meetings. And the whole process can take months, and maybe even years.

There may be other setbacks, as well. For instance, even if the city approves a skate park, there may be last-minute protests that can stall the whole process, such as neighbors concerned about noise level and loitering. So it definitely takes a lot of persistence and patience on your part. But just like when you first learned to skate, you have to hang in there and keep your eyes on the prize. Organizing people to have a skate park built is just as challenging as skateboarding, but also as rewarding. This is because you can see the results of your efforts when the project is finally complete, just like when landing a hard trick.

If you're determined to never give up, your hard work and persistence will eventually pay off.

CHAPTER 4

Fund-Raising

I f your efforts are successful and your city decides to build a skate park, the city itself will often provide only a portion of the funds necessary to complete the project. In this case, your organization may be responsible for raising a good-sized chunk of money.

Considering how hard it is for most young people to scrounge up ten bucks to see a movie, the prospect of raising thousands of dollars might seem impossible. But you're not alone. If you've made it this far then you've definitely had a lot of help from your friends, your family, and your organization. And, as many skate park coalitions have proven before, it's definitely not impossible for a small group of citizens to raise hundreds of thousands of dollars.

For instance, in 1999, the city of Fort Collins, Colorado, approved CASA's request to build a new skate park. But due to budget constraints, the city was

Simple steps, such as setting up a donations and information table like this one, can help you raise money for your park. If you can afford it, you might also consider giving away promotional items—such as T-shirts or bumper stickers—to those who donate above a certain amount. Not only do you get a donation, but whoever wears your shirt or uses your sticker is advertising for your cause.

able to provide only about half of the estimated $200,000 necessary for building the park. CASA and other local citizens' groups were asked to contribute a large amount of the remaining dollars. How did they do it? Mainly by branching out. Instead of relying on just one or two fund-raising techniques, CASA found a wide variety of ways to raise money.

In one instance, the city employed local tile maker and skateboarder John Baise to create handmade tiles to line the upper edge of one of the new skate park's bowls in order to create the effect of an actual backyard swimming pool. Baise worked with CASA to ask corporations, charitable

Fliers like these are a great way to advertise fund-raising events. Make sure you post them everywhere you can—not just where skateboarders hang out, but in local shops, Laundromats, libraries, sports clubs, and music venues. Always get permission to hang your fliers before you put them up. Be aware that hanging fliers on places like telephone poles or other public property without permission might get you a ticket.

organizations, business owners, and individuals to make donations to the skate park project. Those individuals and corporations that gave more than $500 were commemorated with an ornamental tile bearing their name placed in the bowl and on a highly visible outside edge of the skate park. If your park won't include tiles, you might consider selling similar sponsorship space on commemorative benches or placards.

Along with working to secure donations from local businesses, corporations, and individuals, CASA organized a benefit contest to raise money. The contest was held at the existing temporary skate park at a

SOME CITIES WITH SKATE PARKS

Arcata, CA
Asheville, NC
Ashland, OR
Aspen, CO
Baltimore, MD
Belfast, MN
Benicia, CA
Berthoud, CO
Boise, ID
Boulder, CO
Breckenridge, CO
Brigantine, NJ
Brookings, OR
Carbondale, CO
Colorado Springs, CO
Chesapeake, VA
Cheyenne, WY
Chicago, IL
Cincinnati, OH
Corning, NY
Coronado, CA
Coeur d'Alene, ID
Crested Butte, CO
Davis, CA
Dayton, OH
Denver, CO
Donald, OR

East Hampton, NY
Eugene, OR
Fairbanks, AK
Fairfield. CT
Fort Collins, CO
Grand Junction, CO
Green River, WY
Honolulu, HI
Hood River, OR
Huntington Beach, CA
Issaquah, WA
Kansas City, KA
Kenosha, WI
Ketchum, ID
Kirkland, WA
Laramie, WY
Lincoln City, OR
Loraine, OH
Louisville, KY
Mercer Island, WA
Montauk, NY
Mount Vernon, WA
Nantucket, MA
Napa, CA
New York, NY
Orcas Island, WA
Oshkosh, WI

Palo Alto, CA
Petaluma, CA
Philadelphia, PA
Port Orford, OR
Port Townsend, WA
Portland, OR
Salem, OR
Salida, CO
Salt Lake City, UT
San Pedro, CA
Santa Barbara, CA
Santa Cruz, CA
Santa Rosa, CA
Seattle, WA
Sewell, NJ
Silverthorne, CO
Sonoma, CA
Springfield, OH
Talent, OR
Tampa, FL
Telluride, CO
Trinidad, CO
Wausau, WI
Westchester, PA
Wilmington, NC
Yuba City, CA

Skateboarding contests are a good way to raise funds for your skate park. Temporary, portable skating ramps like this one can be rented for your event. You will also need people to act as judges, collect admission and make change, handle crowd control, keep track of the contestants, and hand out the prizes.

local recreation center. Entrants were charged $10, and all of the nearly $1,000 in proceeds went toward construction of the new park. John Baise also worked with the city to produce a special skate park T-shirt, which was sold at the contest.

Along with holding a contest, CASA also held a benefit concert for people of all ages at a local club. Several punk-rock bands played, and half of all the proceeds went directly to the skate park. On a smaller scale, CASA placed several large donation jugs in local skate shops, restaurants, and other businesses. If you create your own donation jugs, make sure to ask permission before leaving one in a place of business, and attach a modified version of your petition information sheet to each container.

These are just a few examples. For your own fund-raising drive, it's important to work with your organization, and especially your local businesspeople, to come up with money-raising ideas that will be effective within your particular community.

Organizing a Skateboarding Contest

Hosting a skate contest is a fun way to raise a large amount of money in a short time. Holding a contest is actually pretty simple once you break it down into small steps. It requires a lot of planning, but you're used to that by now. Here are ten easy steps to throwing a successful contest:

1. Find a good place such as an existing park or even just a parking lot. You can build some of your own simple skateboard obstacles. For help, check out some of the books listed at the back of this book. Since you're most likely working with the local city government, they'll often provide you with a free, safe place to hold your fund-raising contest.

2. Come up with a catchy name for your event. Make some promotional fliers with time, date, location, and cost information just like your fliers for the city council meetings. Also make some eye-catching images. You need to start putting them up at your school and at all the skate shops in the surrounding area at least a month before the event.

3. Talk to your local skate shop owners about donating some products that you can use for contest prizes. You can also ask them to give you a list of some of the major skateboard companies' phone and fax numbers. Fax your contest fliers to several companies, along with an information sheet. Make sure to let them know your event is designed to raise money for a public skate park. Many companies may send you promotional items like shirts, wheels, stickers, trucks, and even complete skateboards to give away as prizes. But you have to contact them at least a month in advance!

4. Make some judging sheets, which are basically just grids for people to write down scores of one to ten for categories like difficulty of tricks, style, and consistency. Have beginner, intermediate, and advanced divisions. And make three copies of the judging sheets for each category (one set for each of the judges). Ask a few older skaters, such as skate shop employees, if they'll volunteer to be judges on the day of the event.

5. Rent some sort of amplifier, preferably a PA loudspeaker or an electric bullhorn. That way people will hear you when you announce who's up next. If you get a PA, make sure it's the kind you can hook a stereo up to. A skate contest isn't a contest without music!

6. Arrive a couple of hours early the day of the event. Set up a table where adult volunteers can sign people up and collect the entry fee. Make sure to spend some time beforehand assigning specific prizes for the top ten winners in each division.

7. Make sure to give each division time to practice. Keep the advanced skaters out of the beginners' practice time.

8. Keep it fun! Skate contests are definitely meant to be fun and to challenge people, not to show off or prove who's the best.

9. Give each contestant two runs of about forty-five seconds each. You'll need one person with a watch to keep track of time. In the end, you should use only the scores from each person's best run.

10. Add up scores at the end of each division and give out the prizes!

Contests are another way to get some press for your skate park project. Before the event, call a local newspaper and invite a reporter to cover the contest. Local newspapers, and sometimes even major skateboard magazines like *Thrasher*, may publish local contest results.

CHAPTER 5

Designing and Building a Skate Park

If you've made it this far and your city has agreed to build a park, then all your effort is beginning to pay off. But you still have a lot of work in front of you. At this stage in the game, there are still many important decisions that need to be made, decisions that can determine whether your city builds a world-class skate park or a $200,000 piece of junk.

The sad reality is that, despite the huge number of parks built in the past few years, not all of them are good. Some of them just plain stink. Good parks are well-designed, functional, and have a smooth skating surface. Bad parks are poorly designed with many flaws (also known as kinks) in the skating surface. Since skateboarders move very fast on small, hard wheels, even the tiniest kinks can cause an accident. So while you've already dedicated a massive amount of time and effort, your skate park quest has really just begun.

Members of CASA work with a consultant to design a skateboard park for the city of Fort Collins, Colorado.

Deciding on the Design

First and foremost, you need to convince your city that the skateboarders should be directly involved in the design process. When skate parks don't turn out well, it's usually because they were built without any input from skaters. Architects and engineers definitely know how to make structurally sound elements, but most of them have no idea what skateboarders really want. Even if your city is reluctant to involve skaters, remind them that you're the ones who will be skating there on a daily basis. If it comes down to it, you may have to demand to be included.

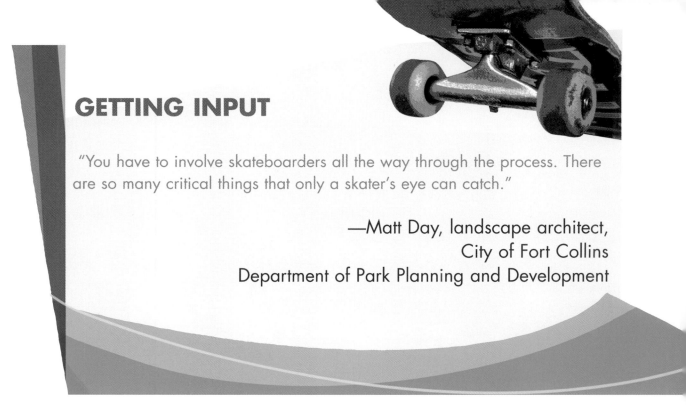

GETTING INPUT

"You have to involve skateboarders all the way through the process. There are so many critical things that only a skater's eye can catch."

—Matt Day, landscape architect,
City of Fort Collins
Department of Park Planning and Development

So, of course, you need to decide what you and the other skaters in your community really do want. Consider having an open meeting and invite every skater in town to participate. Come up with a wish list that asks the skaters to write down what sort of elements they'd like to see in a skate park. Make copies of the wish list form, and let the skaters fill it out. Afterward you can sit down with a few friends and members of your organization, and try to come to some consensus.

Of course, you'll get a lot of different responses, so some of it will be up to you. You have to decide if you want a park with lots of transition, or "tranny," which consists of any skate structure with a curving wall, like quarter-pipes, half-pipes, and bowls. Or maybe you'd prefer a more street-oriented park, with flat ledges, rails, stairs, and gaps. Many parks incorporate both tranny and street elements into their designs, but try to avoid cramming too many obstacles together. Too many obstacles packed too closely together can cause skaters to move in a lot of conflicting lines, which is a major cause of accidents. A well-built park with

Construction begins on Edora Skatepark in Fort Collins, Colorado. At top left, workmen shape the concrete for the bowl. At top right, the foreman consults with the construction workers. At bottom, an artist paints a flame design along the lip of the bowl.

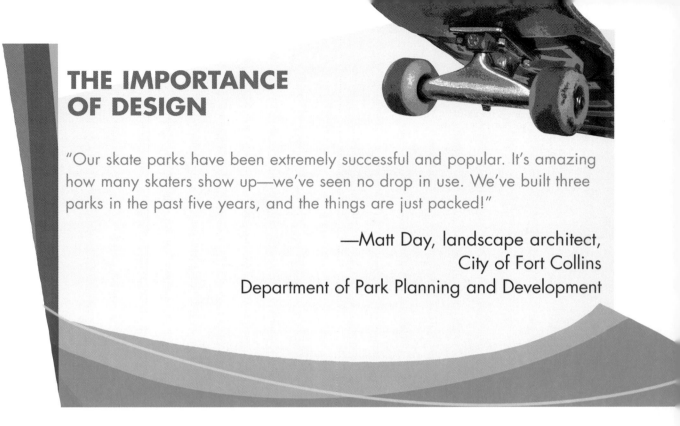

THE IMPORTANCE OF DESIGN

"Our skate parks have been extremely successful and popular. It's amazing how many skaters show up—we've seen no drop in use. We've built three parks in the past five years, and the things are just packed!"

—Matt Day, landscape architect,
City of Fort Collins
Department of Park Planning and Development

good flow will work better than a crowded, cramped one that has too many features.

Working with the Designers

Another helpful step to take involves meeting with the park planners and construction contractors to present city officials with specific examples of well-built parks versus poorly built parks. You can put together a slide show, or show them pictures from skate magazines of what good parks look like.

Secondly, propose that your city create a design team that consists mainly of skateboarders, as well as the city planners and the architects or construction contractors who'll work on the job. Try to choose skaters of different ages and abilities on your team—that way you'll create a park that suits everyone's needs and abilities. At your wish list meeting, you might also hold an informal vote to elect four or five skaters to serve on this design team.

It's also very important to push your city to hire a construction team that has extensive experience building skate parks. Make it very clear that skate park construction is a complicated task, one that requires a great deal of experience and precision, especially if you plan on building bowls.

Custom skate park construction is a growing field, and there are more and more companies doing it (for more information about some of these companies, see one of the other books in this series called *Dream Builders: The World's Best Skateboard Park Creators*). If your city does happen to hire a construction team with no prior skate-park–building experience, ask the city to consider hiring a skate park consultant— someone who has been directly involved in the process before, and who can be on-site every day to give specific advice and suggestions.

If possible, you should also work with the city to arrange for your own regular visits to the construction site. Try to get to know the builders, and make sure they're doing things right—getting the right angles, making surfaces smooth, and working out all the kinks. If you do notice problems, make positive suggestions about what they could improve rather than simply pointing out all their mistakes.

Staying Involved

Once your park actually gets built, it's time to enjoy the fruits of your labor. The biggest reward for all your hard work will be all the fun you'll have skating with your friends. Even though it's time to finally get some serious skating done, you still have a job to do. You've worked hard to claim a place for yourself and your friends, so you have to take care of it. The main thing is to make sure everyone stays safe. Especially when the park first opens, there will be tons of people flying around in a relatively small space.

A good skateboard park can be a great asset to a town or city. It gives kids and skateboarders a place to go, and it decreases skateboard traffic on streets and sidewalks. Like a baseball field or a hiking trail, a skateboard park is one more way to encourage people to get off the couch, get outside, and have fun.

Encourage everyone to watch out for each other and to wear the right safety gear. Even if the city hires a park monitor, you should help enforce the rules and make sure everyone takes care of the park. Clean up after yourselves, and make sure everyone else does the same. If you and your friends take on a sense of personal responsibility for your park (and you encourage others to do the same), generations and generations of future skaters will be able to show and rip without ever having to worry about getting shut down.

It's also important to stay involved with your skateboard coalition. Also, depending on the size of your town or city, one skate park may not be enough to accommodate all the skaters. Now that you know how things work, consider lobbying for a second, or even a third, skate park

GLOSSARY

architecture The art and science of designing buildings and parks.

bowl A kind of specialized skateboard ramp with rounded, concave curves all the way around, like a giant cereal bowl.

city council A group of elected officials who make important decisions about city operations.

coalition A group of people that takes action to achieve a common goal.

fund-raising The act of collecting donations to finance a project.

graphic design Promotional art that usually accompanies fliers, books, posters, and advertisements.

grind A trick where you actually grind the bottom of your truck slides on the top edge of an obstacle like a ledge, handrail, or ramp.

half-pipe A ramp with two transitions used in many skate park courses.

kick flip A trick where the side of the foot is used to flip the board one full rotation.

kink A defect in a ramp that is usually the result of poor planning.

local government The ruling body of a small town or city.

ollie The basis for most skate tricks, the ollie is accomplished by snapping the tail of the skateboard down on the ground and then popping the board and your body up into the air.

petition A list of two or more signatures collected to promote a cause.

quarter-pipe A ramp with one transition used in many street skate park courses.

skatestopper A new breed of metal knobs, brackets, spikes, etc., that are placed on ledges, handrails, and other skateable structures in order to prevent skateboarding.

snake run A group of several small bowls linked together in the shape of a long, curving snake.

trucks The metal devices used for attaching wheels to the deck of the skateboard. Trucks are also what make it possible to turn.

FOR MORE INFORMATION

Dreamland Skateparks
960 SE Highway 101, PMB 384
Lincoln City, OR 97367-2622
(503) 577-9277
Web site: http://www.dreamlandskateparks.com

Grindline Skateparks
4056 23rd Avenue SW
Seattle, WA 98106
(206) 932-6414
e-mail: inform@grindline.com
Web site: http://www.grindline.com

Ramptech
14855 Persistence Drive
Woodbridge, VA 22191
(888) RAMPTEC (726-7832)
e-mail: info@ramptech.com
Web site: http://www.ramptech.com

RCMC Custom Cement Skateparks
48 Jefferson Road
Princeton, NJ 08540
(714) 965-1104
e-mail: carje@earthlink.net
Web site: http://www.rcmcsk8parks.com

Site Design Group, Inc.
24 West 5th Street, Suite #203
Tempe, AZ 85281
(480) 894-6797
e-mail: info@sitedesigngroup.com
Web site: http://www.sitedesigngroup.com

Team Pain Skateparks
890 Northern Way, Suite B-2
Winter Springs, FL 32708
(407) 366-9221
Web site: http://www.teampain.com

Web Sites

Due to the changing nature of Internet links, the Rosen Publishing Group, Inc., has developed an online list of Web sites related to the subject of this book. This site is updated regularly. Please use this link to access the list:

http://www.rosenlinks.com/skgu/taac

FOR FURTHER READING

Brooke, Michael. *The Concrete Wave: The History of Skateboarding.* Toronto, ON: Warwick Publishing, 1999.

Davis, Garry, and Craig Steycyk. *Dysfunctional.* Corte Madera, CA: Ginkgo Press, 1999.

Hawk, Tony. *Hawk: Occupation: Skateboarder.* New York: Reagan Books, 2000.

Thrasher magazine. *Thrasher: Insane Terrain.* New York: Universe Publishing, 2001.

BIBLIOGRAPHY

Befearless.com. "How to Launch a Petition Drive." Retrieved November 12, 2003 (http://befearless.blackhammer.com/features/actkit_05.html).

PetitionOnline.com. "Free On-line Petition." Retrieved November 12, 2003 (http://www.PetitionOnline.com/create_petition.html).

The Plan by Consolidated Skateboards. Retrieved December 10, 2003 (http://www.skatepark.org/Propaganda/Public_Parks/theplan.html).

Skatepark.org. "Fundraising." Retrieved December 10, 2003 (http://www.skatepark.org/Fundxraising).

Skatepark.org. "Resources in Propaganda: Quotes." Retrieved November 12, 2003 (http://www.skatepark.org/Propaganda/Quotes).

Skatepark.org. "Resources in Propaganda: Statistics." Retrieved November 29, 2003 (http://www.skatepark.org/Propaganda/Statistics).

Skateparkdesign.com. "Statistics for Skateparks." Retrieved November 12, 2003 (http://www.skateparkdesign.com/statistics.html).

INDEX

About the Author

Justin Hocking lives and skateboards in New York City. He is also an editor of the book *Life and Limb: Skateboarders Write from the Deep End*, published in 2004 by Soft Skull Press.

Credits

Cover, pp. 4, 7, 10, 13, 25, 28 Nancy Opitz; p. 11 © Gabe Palmer/Corbis; p. 15 http://www.petitiononline.com; pp. 18 (left), 35 (right) Courtesy of Matt Day; pp. 18 (right), 35 (left), 35 (bottom) Courtesy of John Baise; p. 21 © Jeff Greenberg/The Image Works; p. 33 Courtesy of Jason Stutzman; p. 38 © Tony Donaldson/Icon SMI/The Rosen Publishing Group

Designer: Les Kanturek; Editor: Nicholas Croce;
Photo Research: Fernanda Rocha